My Sistahcode

A Queens Journal For The Soul

By

Janita Jones

Copyright © 2020 by Janita Jones

All rights reserved. No part of this book may be used or reproduced by any means, graphic, electronic, or mechanical, including photocopying, recording, taping or by any information storage retrieval system without the written permission of the publisher except in the case of brief quotations embodied in critical articles and reviews.

All characters appearing in this work are fictitious. Any resemblance to real persons, living or dead is purely coincidental.

ISBN: 978-0-578-70631-3

TABLE OF CONTENTS

ACKNOWLEDGEMENT 1

INTRODUCTION 2

My Daily Thoughts 4

- Day 1: Power of I AM 6
- Day 2: Know Thyself 11
- Day 3: Speak it into existence 16
- Day 4: My Fitted Shoes 20
- Day 5: Grab your Crown 26
- Day 6 The Throne: 32
- Day 7: Meditation 38
- Day 8: Stay, Think and Feel Positive 46
- Day 9: Have an Attitude of Gratitude..... 52
- Day 10: Boss Up 58
- Day 11: BeYouTiFul 64
- Day 12: Feed your Mind............................ 70

Day 13: Queendom 76

Day 14: Prayerful 82

Day 15: Stay Awake 90

Day 16: Unstoppable 96

Day 17: Superwoman 102

Day 18: Be Fearless 108

Day 19: Unbreakable 114

Day 20: SistahCode Pledge 120

Day 21: Revelation 126

INSPIRATION MESSAGE FROM MY PARENTS 132

MY SISTAHCODE MISSION 134

DEDICATION 135

ACKNOWLEDGEMENT

I will first start off by giving God all the glory and honor for his protection and direction; I am extremely blessed and highly favored. I am grateful and thankful for my parents whom I love unconditionally, they are my rock. They showed me how to wear my crown as a daughter. My children are my world; they keep me grounded to stay focused on the vision. I will continue to push hard towards my goals for them and also for my brother, who has been immensely supportive of me (this is the crown of a mother and a sister). A special thanks to my DCM whom I have known since my teenage life and the love is still there, thank you so much for your encouraging words and motivation- *"DJM Empire-Pressing Forward."* Special shout out to all of my family members and friends. I love you all dearly.

I would like to acknowledge my co-author DN Miller who took the vision and ran with it with no hesitation. As I always say, "you're the bomb." I give thanks to the My Sistahcode queens for the sisterly support and each one of my state-holders. Let's continue to support one another with positive energy and encouraging words. We will continue to follow the mission and vision as God leads us. To everyone I know or have known throughout my years of life, a special thanks to you as well. It is a blessing to meet people - stepping out of my comfort zone. To the companies. I have worked for, I specially thank you because, due to my career, I learned to wear my crown as an employee and as a leader.

Bless Up and continue to stay focused!!

Crown on, Queens.

INTRODUCTION

This Queen's journal is written to inspire, encourage, empower and motivate all queens, remind them that they are queentiful (beautiful), and teach them to wear their multiple crowns while sitting on their throne. The vision of the journal came to the surface during the reinvention and renaming of the SistahCode group. A brief history: On August 21, 2015, my group page was created as Sistah2Sistah Network. The name was changed at least 3 times until I came up with My SistahCode. This vision was sitting right in front of me in 2015; unfortunately, I had faced many challenges and did not have the support to carry through. Most importantly, I did not have the right crown to push this vision into existence. In 2019, I decided to wear my fitted red stilettos and these shoes gave me the strength to walk by faith and not by sight, in addition, my support system was there cheering me along and we are the DJM Empire, "pressing forward." If you look closely at the group page, you will see a pair of red stilettos next to the name. These shoes have given me the strength to walk in the will of God and trust in him. My support partner, whom I love dearly (my DCM), kept encouraging me to press forward with my vision. With that being said, I am now taking the time to share my Queen's journal on how I had to wear multiple crowns and overcome different events in my lifetime. I pray that this self-help journal will positively influence your thoughts and view of life. Most importantly, do not give up on your dreams. Stay inspired and be around a strong support of queens who will motivate you to do better. I must say the group is surrounded by encouraging queens and that the state-holders have raised their expectations. I am confident that you will see so many views of your different crowns.

My Daily Thoughts

I am free and happy.

I am loving and kind.

I am compassionate.

I am strong.

I am more than enough.

I am blessed and highly favored.

I am a millionaire Queen.

I am thankful.

I am unstoppable.

I am magnificent.

I am wonderfully made.

I am selfless.

I am me.

I am above and not beneath.

I am a woman of God.

I am who I say I am.

I am thankful for life.

I am one of a kind.

I am fantastic.

I am a beautiful QUEEN.

Day 1

Focus of the Day: Power of I AM "The Beginning"

Good Day Queen & Bless Up!

Welcome to day 1. This day is just the beginning and I am so thankful you took the time out to start your journal. As a Queen, this day will bring in something that will give you hope. Today we are going to focus on the power of I AM…. As a queen, it is very crucial to speak with the power of "I AM a QUEEN." I'm sure it felt powerful when you said it. We'll do a challenge or activity together. Now, look into the mirror and say, "I AM a Queen" three times. Say it with confidence and no cheating, Queen. You have to say it three times in the mirror.

Challenge: Here are my 3 I AM statements

1. I AM A QUEEN.
2. I AM BLESSED AND HIGHLY FAVORED
3. I AM A MILLIONAIRE

Did you notice the excitement in your voice? I am sure it was a good feeling to speak with the power of "I AM." If you understand the power of I AM, it will definitely take you to the next day. All-day continue to say this and of course, you can say it in silence. It needs to be in your heart and not just your mouth.

Quote:

"A queen should be like her crown, bright and shining" - Jaquan Anderson

"A queen is confident in her ability to gain respect on all levels." – Amelia Johnson

Bible Verse: The book of Genesis is powerful with the word "I AM."

I AM…

13:7 "giving you this land;"

15:7 "your shield, do not be afraid;"

17:1 "God almighty;"

22:1 "here;"

26:24 with you and will bless you;

45:12 "Speaking to you;"

Bible Verse: The book of Exodus is powerful with the word 'I AM."

I AM…

3:14 "Who I AM."

Today's Date: _____

Day 2

Focus of the Day: Queen, you must know thyself

Hello Queen & Bless Up!

I hope your first day went well. Today is for you to focus on who you are, "Know thyself." In today's journal, I would like you to be honest with yourself. Only you will know what you wrote in your journal. In order to get through this, you have to know the good and bad about yourself. Honesty is the best policy. Let's call this self-revelation. Identify 3 of your strengths and 3 of your weaknesses and grade them with 10 for good, 5 for okay and 1 for bad. Discover your true identity. Never be afraid of your weaknesses, we all have them and it's okay. I am going to do this with you, see my outcome below,

Challenge:

My strength: A good listener (10)

My weakness: Hard on myself (5)

See, that wasn't so bad, now it is your turn. Once you identify your weaknesses, I would like you to take some time on your resting day and think about what you can do to work on them and write it down in your journal. Be true to yourself and you will get through this as a Queen.

Quote:

"We share the truth because we are at peace within ourselves and peacemakers love the rainbow." - Reva Thompson

"Making one Diva smile can change the world may not the whole world, but their world."- Felicia Sparks-Levi

Bible Verse:

Psalm 139:23 "Search me, O God, and know my heart! Try me and know my thoughts."

Colossians 3:10- "and have put on the new self, which is being renewed in knowledge after the image of its creator."

Today's Date: _____

Day 3

Focus of the Day: Queen, Speak it into existence

Good Day Queen & Bless Up!

So far, you have spoken the word "I AM" into existence by believing and perceiving. Now it is time to achieve. I want you to look back on day 1 and read your three I AM statements. Now, I want you to close your eyes and visualize your statements. Remember, when visualizing each "I AM" statement you have to see it with 20/20 vision. That is, see things with a clear view. When I am in the process of speaking things into existence I always see it as already done. For example, when I was looking for a place - my mindset was that it was already done. "I have a four-bedroom house with one room as my office." Did you see how I spoke of it as something that is already done? This is because I believe that words are truly powerful. It isn't impossible because it is right in front of your eyes. The best part of speaking things into existence is that the word of God acknowledges its power in the verse, *"Death and life are in the power of the tongue; and they that love it shall eat the fruit thereof."* Proverbs 18:21

Quote:

"A theory is just an assumption that things will take place, but through God all things can manifest into existence." - Reva Thompson

Bible Verse:

Genesis 1:27-*So God created man in his own image, in the image of God he created him; male and female he created them.*

Today's Date: _____

Day 4

Focus of the Day: Queen Wear you a fitted shoes

Good Day Queen & Bless Up!

Well, Queens, I have to say, if you're on day 4, you have committed yourself to get through this week and I commend you for it, *"Great Job, Queen."* I would like to start off with the classic quote from Marilyn Monroe, *"Give a girl the right shoes and she can conquer the world."* That is a deep message right there. I remember the first time I read her quote and I said to myself this is powerful and meaningful. So, Queens, you need to get you a pair of fitted shoes that you can wear and conquer the world. My favorite shoes are a pair of red stilettos. I actually have an image of a red pair of stilettos on My SistahCode's group page. My shoes give me faith, and my motto has always been "Walk by faith and not by sight." In my shoes, it does get rough and tough, but I wouldn't exchange anything from the world of my past experience and my current situation. Learn how to wear your size.

Challenge: Wear your shoes today with confidence.

Write down your fitted shoes and how you feel wearing them. Remember you must be confident in wearing your shoes. Start off by using your imagination.

Quote:

"A pair of shoes is a Queen's best friend, but walking in faith is more powerful." - **Janita Jones**

"Queens, when Paul was explaining to the people to dress daily by putting on the full armor of God, he made sure to address how we need to be ready for the battle that comes our way. But to also be prepared knowing that with the peace of God's word in your hearts that we do not have to let the stresses of the world today make us anxious; for you know the Lord if with you so boldly go with God and in spite of the naysayers, make your dreams come true." –**Patricia Jones**

Bible Verse:

2 Corinthians 5:7- "For we walk by faith, not by sight."

Proverbs 3:6- "In all your ways acknowledge him, and he will make your paths straight."

Today's Date: _____

Day 5

Focus of the Day: Grab your crown, Queen

Hey Queen & Bless Up!

Have you ever realized that as Queens, we wear multiple crowns throughout our daily lives? I had the privilege to host a book club on My SistahCode platform and this was my discussion. There are many reasons why we wear many crowns and today's focus is for you to grab your crown. Whatever is on your agenda for today, I say to you humbly, *"Queen, grab your crown and shine."* Never leave your crown at home, your crown is for you to wear with confidence. I am not saying you should be arrogant about your crown, but you'll definitely need to wear it with courage and strength.

Challenge:

How many crowns do you wear a day?

Write it down and describe how you feel when you are wearing your crown.

Here are some examples of the many crowns that Queens wear throughout the week:

1. A crown of a mother

2. A crown of a daughter/sister

3. A crown of a girlfriend/significant other/wife

4. A crown of an entrepreneur

5. A crown of an employee

Quote:

"Us Queens was born to wear a crown..." **DJM Empire**

"Spoil me with royalty because a queen can finance herself." Tyrce Davis

Bible Verse:

Isaiah 54:17 – "No weapon formed against me shall prosper"

Today's Date: _____

Day 6

Focus of the Day: Queen on the Throne

Hello Queen & Bless Up!

Today is a special day to enjoy your throne with your family. Your throne is your home, the place where you lay your head and enjoy being in your space with your family. Sometimes we need that time to relax and enjoy the company of our family. For the last 5 days, you have been wearing the additional crown of following this journal and challenge. *"smile."* Imagine each day you had to wear a different crown on your head. This day you are challenged to do something simple. Before we start off with the challenge, give yourself a pat on the back and a big thanks for pushing through. Be good, be dope and stay on your throne, Queen.

Challenge:

On this day, write down what you enjoy so far and which day benefited you the most. I would challenge you to email your response to your friend and/or self. Go back and review it periodically. Keeping this is like a diary to remind yourself not to go backwards.

Quote:

"Without a Queen, there wouldn't be a King" - **David Macon**

"A Queen must always cherish and protect her throne to stand strong; be a leader to rise and show her princess how to become a Queen." – **Mary Willis**

Bible Verse:

Proverbs 4:9- "She will give you a garland to grace your head and present you with a glorious crown."

Today's Date: _____

Day 7

Focus of the Day: Meditation Time

Hey Queen & Bless Up!

Keep your meditation simple. Learn how to be in a quiet area to connect with your inner-self, become more self-aware. This challenge connects with Day 2 - *"Know Thyself."* To know who you are, meditation is definitely required. Before meditation, say a prayer first, then concentrate on your inner power and focus on the forgiveness of others. A form of forgiveness comes in many shapes and forms The most popular shape that I believe in is forgiving others for your own interest. This forgiveness allows you to move on with your life to let go of the past and hurt. Just like carrying a baggage full of trash; dump the baggage in the waste bin where it belongs. Get rid of all toxicity and unhealthiness. It is time to heal and regain your strength, Queen. Never let anyone control who you are or have power over your thoughts.

Challenge:

Take thirty minutes today and meditate on a positive thought, but remember to pray before meditation.

Write down exactly what you visualized while meditating and pray over it. The more you read it, the more it will come to existence/ life. Learn to speak things into existence during meditation.

Quote:

"A Queen is you. No matter what you look like, no matter what your situation is; as long as you believe in yourself and have the utmost confidence and respect yourself. You are a true Queen. So keep pushing and continue striving and definitely keep that crown on your head." - **David Macon**

"Be a princess with a mind and a queen with an attitude building your own empire" - Janita Jones

"Life can put you in a circle so you have to unbend it just like a paperclip to be on a straight path." -Jaquan Anderson

Bible Verse:

Psalm 19:14- "Let the words of my mouth and the meditation of my heart be acceptable in your sight, O Lord, my rock and my redeemer." ESV

Today's Date: _____

My Beauty Box

There are 21 words hidden in the word search below, the words may be found across, down, diagonally and backwards and can overlap with each other. The hidden words are listed beneath the word search; circle the words in the word search as you find them and cross them out from the list.

```
W N L O V L R W E U R K M Y O F S O N E
E B O N E R A B I B M I Y H S T H P U I
N H R E E U B N A E T T A T L E R T F E
D U M T C E R R R G I A R R U R J E E H
T S V T I Y T I N U G A U O B O N I E T
A T H L E N O A I E O A M W S N T I D W
H L W Y G N F M H N X J G L T O S U Y H
T E V I T I S O P I P O T E P H J N O H
R O T H I N K D B L P E E C L F T I U M
A A A O V D R N P E H C T E O E A V R E
N H M N I J O E R M O H O O D A O E M M
S L U Y T V H E O I D O P S F Q O R I O
P U T I I N N U R T T U V A S R Y S N R
A F I W W O T Q T I S G M E W T N E D I
R I T E O I C O Q S I D N S I I Y C H E
E T I S R T P E O E E H T R W F S X R S
N U N B K O R B L F I R H S I W J D L R
C A N T O V U D E Y I R I O P T O A O S
Y E I H U E N C N V E S A E O E S U O M
P B S H T D D H E A V O A N U H G V E G
```

Baggage	Beautiful	BossUp
Devotion	FeedYourMind	Honor
Hustle	Journal	Memories
Positive	Queendom	Strive
Think	Timeline	Transparency
Unity	Universe	Wisdom
Wish	Workout	Worthy

My Beauty Box

Queen, grab your beauty box?. Here are 21 beauty supplies you should apply in your Beauty Box to get your "BeYouTiFul" day started.

1. Love.
2. Positivity.
3. Strength.
4. Focus.
5. Unity.
6. Thankfulness.
7. Self-Confidence.
8. Faith.
9. Blessing.
10. Kindness.
11. Smiles.
12. Integrity.
13. Character.
14. Worthiness.
15. Wisdom.
16. Devotion.
17. Respect.
18. Memories.
19. Vision.
20. Crown.
21. Confidence.

Day 8

Focus of the Day: Stay Positive, Think Positive and Feel Positive

Hey Queen & Bless Up!

Embarking on a positive journey in your life will generate positive energy. Learn how to stay positive through any challenges and in the midst of any storm that may come your way. There will be many times we might have to face a situation that we least expected. I say to you, learn how to keep yourself motivated, workout, read a word from the book of Proverbs, or stay around a group of positive people. Learn how to pick your friends and associates. You don't always need a plan, sometimes you just need to breathe, trust, let go and see what happens. There are no limits to what you can accomplish, except the limits you place on yourself! Stay strong, think and feel positive, Queen. My motto is to eliminate negative thinkers and folks who always think the worst. Do a sister-friend examination and ask yourself these questions below

1. Do you have a sister-friend who will be honest with you when you are wrong?

2. When was the last time you received an encouraging word from your sister-friend?

3. If you have to rate your girl chat, do you spend more time gossiping or more time encouraging one another?

Challenge: Answer the following questions in your journal;

1. Write down 15 positive things.
2. What are some things that keep you positive when things seem to be falling apart?
3. What is your favorite positive quote that always gets you through a struggle?

Quote:

"Push, Pull, Strive, my Queen is on the Rise" - **David Macon**

"Wear your crown everyday, Queen" - *Janita Jones*

Bible Verse:

Matthew 21:22- "And whatever you ask in prayer, you will receive, if you have faith." **ESV**

Proverbs 18:21-"Death and life are in the power of the tongue, and those who love it will eat its fruits." **ESV**

Today's Date: _____

Day 9

Focus of the Day: Have an Attitude of Gratitude

Hello Queen & Bless Up!

I have seen so many Queens who were in a position of power but lost their crown because of a lack of gratitude. One of the most important rules of life is to have a heart of gratitude and be thankful for the small things you are blessed with. Understand the importance of how small blessings can help you achieve the next level of your life. As soon as you understand the importance of gratitude, the universe will release many more blessings. One thing I have learned in my life journal is understanding how to perceive, achieve and receive my blessings even if it is something as small as a $5 bill - I am so thankful for that $5 that someone gave me as a blessing seed. You have to wake up every day and say, The moment you realize how to be thankful, you will see how your blessings will flow ceaselessly. I'll share an experience with you, even when I had hit rock bottom - I still felt happy to be alive. My attitude has always been a thankful one. An attitude that shows gratitude for being alive.

Challenge: Follow the instructions below and write down your answers in today's journal.

1. Write down 10 things that you are grateful for and why.

2. Be honest with yourself; have you received something small and realized you weren't thankful for it and had to check yourself? If so, write it down and apologize for it.

Quote:

"How you carry yourself reflects on your character… be thankful" - **David Macon**

"It's always nice to have someone in your life that makes you smile even when they're not around." **David Macon**

Bible Verse:

Psalm 118:24 – *"This is the day that the Lord has made; let us rejoice and be glad in it."* **ESV**

Acts 24:3- *"In every way and everywhere, we accept this with all gratitude."* **ESV**

Today's Date: _____

Day 10

Focus of the Day: Boss Up, Queen

Good Day Queen & Bless Up!

Time to boss up, Queen. A boss queen has no other choice but to boss up and reach the next level. A boss queen stays in her own lane and respects the SistahCode and hustle. She knows how to respect herself as well as others on the throne and take no crap. Never expect anything from anyone. You have to go out of your way and go get it. Be a goal digger and accomplish your goals and visions. Put timelines on everything you plan, such as realistic dates. Stick by the date you come up with and fulfill it. While you are building your goals, make sure you go back and check your accomplishments quarterly. Learn how to pull others up as you are reaching a higher level. If you fail, do not get discouraged or give up, just press forward. As Boss Queens, we don't give up easily, we stay focused on our goals. At the end of the day, Boss Queens, are going to win, so keep your crown on sis. Remember, our crown might tilt a bit, but it is designed to fit our head. Same vision, same goals, and same directions Boss Up.

<u>Challenge:</u> Follow the instructions below and write down your answers in today's journal.

1. Write down your short term and long term goals.
3. For each goal, give yourself a realistic date to accomplish them.

4. Go back and see your progress monthly.
5. Every milestone is a success.

Quote:

"How you carry yourself reflects on your character" - **David Macon**

"The Definition of a true queen is a strong woman who loves herself and shines amongst those who have doubts." - ***Javontae Collins***

Bible Verse:

Proverbs 21:20- *"Precious treasure and oil are in a wise man's dwelling, but a foolish man devours it."* **ESV**

John 10:10- *"The thief comes only to steal and kill and destroy. I came that they may have life and have it abundantly."* **ESV**

Today's Date: _____

Day 11

Focus of the Day: BeYouTiFul

Good Day Queen & Bless Up!

Being you is the most beautiful thing you can ever accomplish. I know it is a great feeling and there is strength in being BeYouTiFul, Queen. There isn't any competition when loving yourself, unconditionally. You should always be yourself despite what others might say about you. You realize what is important and what isn't. You learn to care less about what other people think of you and more about what you think of yourself. You realize how far you've come and you remember when you thought things were such a mess and that you'd never recover. People will always be quick to be judgmental on others and if you spend more time thinking about what people feel or think of you, it will stop your progress. Wake up every day saying, *"I am Beautiful with my crown on."* I promise you are going to love the vibration of BeYouTiFul coming out of your mouth. Don't wait, go ahead and say it daily. Get started today and every day. You are seriously beyoutiful!!!

Challenge: Follow the instructions below and write down your answers in today's journal.

1. Write down what makes you a beautiful person inside and out
2. Are you confident within yourself and outer appearance?

3. Do you need to wear expensive clothing to feel or look beautiful?
4. How will you rate your outer appearance with 10 being the highest and 1 being the lowest?
6. Now re-evaluate your answers and write down what you need to spend more focus on.

"To love myself, is to love the world" -**DNMiller**

"I am a beautiful Queen, not conceited but confident in me" - **Janita Jones**

Bible Verse:

Proverbs 11:22 - "Like a gold ring in a pig's snout is a beautiful woman without discretion." **ESV.**

1 Timothy 2:9 – "Likewise also that women should adorn themselves in respectable apparel, with modesty and self-control, not with braided hair and gold or pearls or costly attire." **ESV**

Today's Date: _____

_____
_____
_____
_____
_____
_____
_____
_____
_____
_____
_____
_____
_____
_____
_____
_____
_____

Day 12

Focus of the Day: Feed your Mind with Wisdom, Knowledge and Understanding

Good Day Queen & Bless Up!

I'd rather have wisdom, knowledge and understanding than money in my hands. This might seem ridiculous to you or unbelievable, but once I break it down for you, hopefully, you can understand why I feel this way. Let me clearly explain it to you in layman terms. If you have the wisdom to strategize a business plan that will bring in cash flow, and the knowledge to understand the blueprint and an understanding of the foundation, you have literally built yourself a financial house of income. You have to learn how to feed your mind.with wisdom Have you ever wondered why a person who was blessed with millions ended up losing it within 5 to 10 years? Queen, the reason is because they lacked this trio.concept Learn how to stay ahead by feeding your mind with information that can help you with your cash flow. It literally takes multiple streams of income to live a normal life. I am sure you have a clear understanding of this concept now- it is now time for the challenge.

Challenge: Time for you to build your financial house with a blueprint, foundation and a plan of action. Describe how each one of the following below impact your financial house. Now draw a picture of your new home with financial freedom.

1. Wisdom,
2. Knowledge, and
3. Understanding.

Quote:

"You don't have to be great to get started, but you have to get started to get great." - **Les Brown**

"One Queen doesn't let another Queen fall." --Tracy Beck-Turner

Bible Verse:

Proverbs 1:7- *"The fear of the LORD [is] the beginning of knowledge: [but] fools despise wisdom and instruction."* **KJV.**

Matthew 7:7- 8 – *"Ask, and it shall be given you; seek, and ye shall find; knock, and it shall be opened unto you."* **KJV.**

Today's Date: _____

Day 13

Focus of the Day: Your Queendom

Good Day Queen & Bless Up!

Today is the day you must honor your Queendom and understand who you are in your palace. Accept your queenship, sis. This is the time for you to accept all situations. Feel comfortable with your walk; this is just the beginning. You were born to be a Queen, therefore, accept all of your flaws and hiccups. You are allowed to make mistakes and correct them by acceptance. There will always be some unexpected news but it takes you to stand on your Queendom and give birth to the new Queen that you are. Devote yourself to a new you and allow yourself to live and learn. Rise, Queen and feel free. You may not be able to control every situation and its outcome, but you can control your attitude and how you deal with it. Every situation in life is temporary. So, when life is good, make sure you enjoy and receive it abundantly. And when life is not good, remember that it will not last forever and better days are coming.

<u>Challenge</u>: Follow the instructions below and write down your answers in today's journal.

1. Acknowledge: Write down 5 mistakes you have made in the past week.

2. Accept: Receive it and Honor it with Integrity.
3. Prevention: Create a plan on how to prevent this from happening all over again.

Quote:

"It's the Queen in me"- **Vivian Blair-Housen**

"King come and get your Queen"- **Vivian Blair-Housen**

Bible Verse:

2Timothy 2:25- *Do your best to present yourself to God as one approved, a worker who has no need to be ashamed, rightly handling the word of truth.* –ESV

Today's Date: _____

Day 14

Focus of the Day: Be Prayerful

Hello Queen & Bless Up!

Prayers work Queen. I am always in prayer mode. I wake up being thankful for each day. I tell you to do the same thing. You have to learn how to get into prayer mode and start praying for God's direction and his leadership. Without prayers, we are lost; if you want a business and to become wise, ask God to lead the way. Go back and look at day 12 and ask for wisdom, knowledge and understanding. When was the last time you sat in a quiet place and just prayed out of gratitude for being alive? Be prayerful and stay geared up. When I have nobody to turn to, I meditate and pray. You have to believe it, receive it and proclaim it.

Challenge: Find a quiet area and take time out to pray. I challenge you to start your daily prayer regimen and build a relationship with God. Find a specific time and dedicate it to developing a prayerful relationship with God; seize every opportunity to give him all the thanks and honor. He is the only way maker that can lead you through any obstacles that you are facing.

Quote:

"How you carry yourself is most important by keeping your crown up and not down." – **Nikki Reed**

"We, as people of God will never understand why we are shifted, but if we trust in God all the way and walk in our faith of shoes, he will direct our footsteps. He will never leave us without guidance. Trust in the Lord wholeheartedly and not your own understanding." – **Janita Jones**

Bible Verse:

John 1 5:7- *"If you abide in me, and my words abide in you, ask whatever you wish, and it will be done for you."* ESV

Today's Date: _____

My 20/20 Vision

There are 21 words hidden in the word search below, the words may be found across, down, diagonally and backwards and can overlap with each other. The hidden words are listed beneath the word search; circle the words in the word search as you find them and cross them out from the list.

```
D S T M M E N E R E T D M F N A H A H T N M
T O R E R E D L S A C S E T O H N C E N I R
Y T J T S W G U W E E R A I I A I F R E H E
T D Y N T W S H T H X N A T T I O O O M T A
Y E N R U O J S Y I O A P S A L M O L N I Y
F A R S I G H T E D T P M E C U D I T R A T
J N G E O C R A I L D T E I I R M M H E F I
W G I R D I H H D A R E A F N T I A N C T R
D E T H G I S R A E N A M E U A E I O S T G
F B I T A L A O O I O O E A M L T U O I N E
S T A R B N T T I D M N I F M T N I A D N T
E M U D R E A M B I G T H G O T Y E O H I N
E A D I C E E N E S D O M S C I D J S N T I
D I T L N R T N O I T N E V E R P I N S C T
I E P O A E H E O E H V O I G E R O S R N D
S T L A T P O U D S L H N N S A U E E M N A
T I S O A X N R I I S A W T L N G A A U T A
A M M O D N E E U Q T Y O A M E T N E I Y I
N O S C I N S I O T A T R F O I E T I M N R
C T E O M Y T E I E R L C C V I O E E O K L
E H T S I R Y T L I B M A E D M C O U W R I
O Y D N O I T A T I M I L O N L S E T O M F
```

Attitude	Communication	Creative
Crown	Discernment	Dreambig
Examination	Faith	Farsighted
Fearless	Honesty	Hopefulness
Integrity	Journey	NearSighted
NoLimitation	Prevention	Psalm
Queendom	SeeDistance	Timothy

20/20 Vision- this journal was published in 2020 which means clear vision. Be a visionary Queen.

Here are some items you need to add to your 20/20 prescription

1. Dream Big
2. No limitation
3. Faith
4. See distance
5. Discernment
6. Creativity
7. Hopefulness
8. Fearless
9. Nearsighted
10. Farsighted

Day 15

Focus of the Day: Stay Awake

Hello Queen & Bless Up!

Stay awake and focused on your goals and benefits instead of focusing on someone else's. Otherwise, your goal is going to sink. People who see you moving far will always be your number one cheerleaders or supporters. So I say to you, Queen; stay awake, ignore all the noise and critics that will try to distract you. Have you ever noticed that anytime you take one step forward, there's always someone trying to take you two steps backward? This can come in the form of negativity, distraction, drama, foolishness. At a young age, I was blessed to experience these types of tactics from so many people and still do as a grown woman. I've been in a relationship where my so-called partner felt insecure because I was ambitious and wanted to press forward. Sometimes we get lost in the worldly world and lose focus on ourselves. Stay awake Queen and make sure you have someone on your corner who will support your vision and dreams. We have one life to live and I say to you, live it with big dreams and goals, and most importantly, have someone who will be your number one supporter while you're working towards your dream.

Challenge: Follow the instructions below and write down your answers in today's journal.

1. How do you stay focused while multitasking on many projects?
2. Do you have a cheerleader or supporter?
3. What does your vision board look like?

Quote:

"A Queen must attach herself to a quality that sets her apart from others" - **David Macon**

"Self-motivation is the best motivation, never give up nor give in, Queen." -**David Macon**

"A queen should continue to press forward and birth her visions." -***Tyrœ Davis)***

Today's Date: _____

Day 16

Focus of the Day: Be Unstoppable, Queen

Hello Queen & Bless Up!

Be like a female lioness, unstoppable. There are many traits of a lioness, such as her strength, her courage, and her ability to protect her cubs. Never give people the opportunity to question your next move/plan of action; let them see how determined you are and how you are unstoppable despite what they toss your way. People will try to attack you and prey on your strength, but be that wild lioness and stay strong with your chin up and protect your character with an unstoppable tenacity, Queen. It is sad to say that you will be under the microscope because of your strength and courage. Stay firm and give them something to talk about even more. Be a go-getter and do not give in. Never give up! Reach inside, give it all you've got, as long as you're alive you can keep on trying. Discover how strong you are, don't let anything or anyone bring you down, instead be someone who lifts others up by not giving up and inspiring others with all you achieved. Say this with power, "I AM UNSTOPPABLE."

Challenge: Follow the instructions below and write down your answers in today's journal.

1. Describe what makes you unstoppable.

2. When was the last time you had to press forward even though you were tired?
3. Describe what technique you utilize to stay ahead.
4. Name 3 things you will do to be unstoppable.

Quote:

"A true Queen will straighten another's Queen's crown when she sees her sister's crown tilted." –Tracy Beck-Turner

"Let nothing hold you back. Continue to smell the roses, Queen." – **Nikki Reed**

Bible Verse:

Isaiah 55:8-9–*"For my thoughts are not your thoughts, neither are your ways my ways, declares the Lord. For as the heavens are higher than the earth, so are my ways higher than your ways and my thoughts than your thoughts."* ESV

Genesis 1:27–*"So God created man in his own image, in the image of God he created him; male and female he created them."* ESV

Today's Date: _____

Day 17

Focus of the Day: My Superwoman Power

Hello Queen & Bless Up!

Start off with your superwoman power. Discover who you are by recognizing the superwoman power equipment within. Today is the day you dress up as a superwoman by believing in yourself. Your character and image should be so secure that it matches your outer appearance. Be a product of your superwoman power, take your inner strength to protect yourself. A superwoman possesses super strength and doesn't give up easily. A superwoman wears no mask because she has nothing to hide. Be yourself, wear your true identity very well. My first time experiences my superwoman power I remember how easy it became to walk with my head up and know who I am regardless of what others might feel or think. Who cares? There are going to be many people who will be intimidated because of your superwoman power, but I say to you Queen, stay strong and continue to be that superhero. I have read many self-help books to help me with my superwoman power and believe me, as long as I am determined to nurture it, it will continue to grow. You can have many degrees and be very intelligent, but if you lack the superwoman power, you will always be a target.

Challenge: Follow the instructions below and write down your answers in today's journal.

1. Name three of the superwoman powers you carry within.
2. How do you use each superwoman power when you are under attack?
3. Describe two incidents where you felt you were powerless and why. What will you do to prevent this from happening again?

Quote:

"A Queen must accept her flaws; fix whatever is broken inside and feel good about herself and know that she is a valuable, worthy queen." **David Macon**

"A Queen status shows not by the crown that she wears but the throne that she sits upon." **Geneva Simuel**

Bible Verse:

Psalm 46:5 *"God is in the midst of her; she shall not be moved; God will help her when morning dawns."*

Today's Date: _____

Day 18

Focus of the Day: Be Fearless

Hello Queen & Bless Up!

We all make life mistakes and errors, we must acknowledge them, learn from them and use them as stepping stones to become fearless Queens. Today is the day to move with force, attack your goals and be fearless. Sometimes the smallest step ends up being the biggest step you made in life. Tiptoe if you must, at least you have taken the very first step. There are no limits to what you can accomplish, except the limits placed by your own thinking. If you learn how to program yourself as an incredible queen who is not afraid to step out of the box, I am sure you will succeed. It is all in the mind, walking fearlessly and with superwoman strength. The hardest part is getting started. People tend to observe your character and reactions to situations, but trust me, if you show a bit of fear, people will treat you as a nervous wreck. The mission is to create an environment that will give you an image of a self-confident Queen who knows what she wants and is not afraid to go out there and get it. Wake up in the morning and be fearless, Queen. Stretch yourself to become fearless. Remember, self-motivation is the best motivation, never give up nor give in because of fear.

Challenge:

Take 15 minutes to meditate and think about how you can overcome fear by walking with confidence. Once you finish meditating, write down whatever comes to your mind. This is where you just free-flow on your thoughts and feelings. Now write it down and then go back and revisit it 30 minutes later with fresh eyes. This will give you a good perspective on what you feel internally, and you'll understand how to work on it.

Quote:

"Confidence is in you, bring it to life by doing what you love." – **Nikki Reed**

"Be confident all the time not just some of the time."- **DN Miller**

Bible Verse:

Psalm 27:2- *Of David. The Lord is my light and my salvation; whom shall I fear? The Lord is the stronghold of my life; of whom shall I be afraid?* **ESV**

Today's Date: _____

Day 19

Focus of the Day: Unbreakable

Hello Queen & Bless Up!

No matter what knocks you down in life, get back up and keep going. Never give up and settle for less. Great blessings are a result of great perseverance. We may encounter many defeats, but we must not be defeated. As I was writing today's journal, I watched the George Floyd Memorial Service and listened to Rev. Al Sharpton who delivered the eulogy. He said, *"Get your knees off our neck."* I saw so many people in unity fighting in wholeness for justice. Don't settle for mediocrity in life. Stand up for your life and stand for what is right. This is the life Do not let anyone stop you from moving to your next movement. We need to get up, breathe and speak out in truth and facts. Do not let anything in life stop you and remember what Al Sharpton said, *"Get your knees off our neck."* Be undefeated and unbreakable!

Challenge: Follow the instructions below and write down your answers in today's journal.

Write down 10 things that make you strong and why.

Quote:

"Shine brighter than the stars in the midst of darkness." -DN Miller

<u>Bible Verse:</u>

Isaiah 61:3- *"to console those who mourn in Zion, to give them beauty for ashes, the oil of joy for mourning, the garment of praise for the spirit of heaviness that they may be called trees of righteousness, the planting of the Lord."* ESV

Revelation 21:1- *Then I saw a new heaven and a new earth, for the first heaven and the first earth had passed away, and the sea was no more.* ESV

Today's Date: _____

Day 20

Focus of the Day: My SistahCode Pledge

Hello Queen & Bless Up!

Today I want you to understand the SistahCode. Be very picky with your circle of friends. The reason behind this is to avoid drama. As a queen who understands the code, you must avoid drama and stay drama free. You are a reflection of your friends, so keep in mind to stay away from the drama. If you have a group of friends who are always in a mess, backbiting and gossiping, it is a reflection of who you are and the code you live by. Like attracts like, who you spend most of your time with is the type of person you'll become. My SistahCode has a pledge that we abide by as a true sisterhood, below is an example.

"I, (Janita Jones) will be a respectable queen and will be a sister supporter amongst my sisters. I will not be cruel or dishonest with My SistahCode queens. I will not bring in negativity and it is my responsibility to be a positive influencer and an all-time inspirer." You definitely need to have rules amongst your circle of friends to keep the friendship and love going. This way there will never be any conflict or misunderstanding. Stay focused on positive ENERGY and be ANTI Toxic Energy.

Challenge: Follow the instructions below and write down your answers in today's journal.

Write a sister-ship pledge for your group of friends that you will collaborate with and agree upon. Once you have all agreed to the pledge, follow up in 30 days to see if you have made progress within your circle of friends or maybe you just have that one special best friend you'll like to create a pledge for.

Quote:

"A Queen never competes because we are already the winner."- **DN Miller**

Bible Verse:

Numbers 30:2-"If a man vows a vow to the Lord, or swears an oath to bind himself by a pledge, he shall not break his word. He shall do according to all that proceeds out of his mouth." **ESV**

Today's Date: _____

Day 21

Focus of the Day: Revelation

Hello Queen & Bless Up!

As I look back, I couldn't wait to turn 21 years old—the legal age to party (LOL). Now looking at this at a mature age, I have come to realize that life will take its course. Every cycle of life has its timing. Therefore, I urge you not to rush your lifetime. Let life take its course, experience it, accept your failures and learn from it. Continue to enjoy life with caution. You have to walk at your own timing, not your parents', relatives', siblings or friends' timing. Don't move in the same direction as others, recreate yourself to walk in a different direction. Be the opposite. Do not accept the easy roads that life brings to your attention and learn to have your own identity. Be the master of your own image rather than letting others define your image and character, be who you are. Everybody wants the best in life, but not the struggle that comes with it. "Never go back to what broke you, be strong enough to walk away and be patient enough to wait for what you deserve... it's coming!" Focus on your focus. You are amazing and don't ever be afraid to be amazing. Stay FOCUSED on the VISION!!!

Challenge: Follow the instructions below.

Write down your experience and come up with a personal pledge. In your personal pledge to yourself discover some of the new adventures you learned while writing in your journal. Go back and look at your progress after 30 days. Queen, you ROCK!!! "CROWN ON"

Quote:

"Be Royal in your own fashion, Act like a Queen to be treated like one. The way you carry yourself will also determine how you are treated! For A Queen respects herself and inspires the same sentiment in others!" **- Janita Jones**

"To all beautiful queens, this world is cold, mean, hateful and deceitful. You got to be on your guard at all times. Don't be around anyone who doesn't have the same outlook on life as you do. Stay moving forward, positive and not looking backwards, negative. **– Jesse Jones**

Today's Date: _____

My Daily Thoughts

There are 21 words hidden in the word search below, the words may be found across, down, diagonally and backwards and can overlap with each other. The hidden words are listed beneath the word search; circle the words in the word search as you find them and cross them out from the list.

```
O E E N O I T A N I M R E T E D C D C
Q N O A N S E S S L A G O A L S S A Y
C E T A N O I S S A P M O C D D B E T
G D C N O N W O R C N S E K S R O C H
G R A T I T U D E I W O T E C A I I Y
B V D A C F E A O E B E I V R P W V S
W S S C O S L F O O O D H T S I O F E
O T P C C E R S E E B F Y O A T E E L
E O U O E G N E L L A H C C P I H I F
N S T M L Q R A D I G S M C O E D L I
O M S P M U E L R S B R E V O R P E N
R B I L I E E W I C N U G I D B A B M
H V I I H E F A N T A S T I C S Y C I
T E A S M N I N V T T T R L L U K L
H E L H I O J I T S S E I A I M A E A
N P E B O A S L I Z F S D B I A G I O
C T E G I S R I E A R C S I E I A M O
U I T E D B T F F O R G I V E N E S S
E A H C I I J C O N F I D E N C E S A
```

Accomplish	Belief	Bible
Challenge	Compassionate	Confidence
CrownOn	Determination	Drive
Fantastic	Focus	Forgiveness
Goals	Gratitude	Hope
IAm	Mediation	Proverbs
Queen	Throne	Thyself

INSPIRATION MESSAGE FROM MY PARENTS

Janita is a very hard working young lady. She's very smart and intelligent. During her teenage days she was not sure what she wanted to do with her life. She was not doing too well at all in her school days and teenage life. I proposed if she graduated from High School that I would buy her a car. She graduated from high school and I stuck with my promise. I believed in her and told her whatever you do, be the best of it. Ever since then Janita has been striving for excellence; she is independent and very focused on what she wants in life. She is my first and I love her dearly. "Daughter continue to strive for excellence and keep your eyes on the prize, I love you."

Love Dad!

My daughter was introduced to God when she was a young girl, and her FAITH in God has grown deeper and stronger as an adult. She gives God all the Glory, for she recognizes all things through GOD is possible. I greatly appreciate my daughter (Janita) strength, and ability to never give up on any of her accomplishments. She is always striving to achieve and escalate to the next level in life through her independence. Her determination never been built or centered on her own success, but she loves to encourage others in succeeding in life too. She has shown excellence in leadership management, supervision and most of all as a family member. She always put family first. I love you my daughter and son, so proud of you both, and my grandchildren.

Love Mom!

MY SISTAHCODE MISSION

My SistahCode mission is to empower women of all ages and color to the next generation of becoming future leaders and business owners. The focus is to overcome the challenges of negative influences and create a positive change within themselves by instilling in them the knowledge and power of wearing multiple crowns, *"walk by faith and not by sight."*

Follow us on Facebook and Instagram at My SistahCode and visit us at **www.mysistahcode.com**.

DEDICATION

This journal is dedicated to ALL Queens on My SistahCode group page and women of all ages who are striving to succeed. Don't give up even when life appears that you are drowning, get up and swim again. We all have choices in life. Stay encouraged in the word (Bible) and believe that anything is possible with God. Never give people the power to direct your footsteps or your faith. My late aunt Delores "Rest in Peace" always reminded me not to give up on my dreams. This journal is for every Queen who believes in themselves. Be around people who will keep you motivated. I am delighted to dedicate this book to ALL Queens of ALL ages to stay focused and remember nothing is too hard for our GOD.

BlessUp, Queens!!